Numa

Conversation Pieces

A Small Paperback Series from Aqueduct Press

Subscriptions available: www.aqueductpress.com

1. The Grand Conversation
   Essays by L. Timmel Duchamp
2. With Her Body
   Short Fiction by Nicola Griffith
3. Changeling
   A Novella by Nancy Jane Moore
4. Counting on Wildflowers
   An Entanglement by Kim Antieau
5. The Traveling Tide
   Short Fiction by Rosaleen Love
6. The Adventures of the Faithful Counselor
   A Narrative Poem by Anne Sheldon
7. Ordinary People
   A Collection by Eleanor Arnason
8. Writing the Other
   A Practical Approach
   by Nisi Shawl & Cynthia Ward
9. Alien Bootlegger
   A Novella by Rebecca Ore
10. The Red Rose Rages (Bleeding)
    A Short Novel by L. Timmel Duchamp
11. Talking Back: Epistolary Fantasies
    edited by L. Timmel Duchamp
12. Absolute Uncertainty
    Short Fiction by Lucy Sussex

13. Candle in a Bottle
    A Novella by Carolyn Ives Gilman

14. Knots
    Short Fiction by Wendy Walker

15. Naomi Mitchison: A Profile of Her Life and Work
    A Monograph by Lesley A. Hall

16. We, Robots
    A Novella by Sue Lange

17. Making Love in Madrid
    A Novella by Kimberly Todd Wade

18. Of Love and Other Monsters
    A Novella by Vandana Singh

19. Aliens of the Heart
    Short Fiction by Carolyn Ives Gilman

20. Voices From Fairyland:
    The Fantastical Poems of Mary Coleridge,
    Charlotte Mew, and Sylvia Townsend Warner
    Edited and With Poems by Theodora Goss

21. My Death
    A Novella by Lisa Tuttle

22. De Secretis Mulierum
    A Novella by L. Timmel Duchamp

23. Distances
    A Novella by Vandana Singh

24. Three Observations and a Dialogue:
    Round and About SF
    Essays by Sylvia Kelso and a correspondence
    with Lois McMaster Bujold

25. The Buonarotti Quartet
    Short Fiction by Gwyneth Jones

26. Slightly Behind and to the Left
    Four Stories & Three Drabbles by Claire Light

27. Through the Drowsy Dark
    Short Fiction and Poetry
    by Rachel Swirsky

28. Shotgun Lullabies
    Stories and Poems by Sheree Renée Thomas

29. A Brood of Foxes
    A Novella by Kristin Livdahl

30. The Bone Spindle
    Poems and Short Fiction by Anne Sheldon

31. The Last Letter
    A Novella by Fiona Lehn

32. We Wuz Pushed
    On Joanna Russ and Radical Truth-Telling
    by Brit Mandelo

33. The Receptionist and Other Tales
    Poems by Lesley Wheeler

34. Birds and Birthdays
    Stories by Christopher Barzak

35. The Queen, the Cambion, and Seven Others
    Stories by Richard Bowes

36. Spring in Geneva
    A Novella by Sylvia Kelso

37. The XY Conspiracy
    A Novella by Lori Selke

38. Numa
    An Epic Poem
    by Katrinka Moore

39. Myths, Metaphors, and Science Fiction:
    Ancient Roots of the Literature of the Future
    Essays by Sheila Finch

About the Aqueduct Press Conversation Pieces Series

The feminist engaged with sf is passionately interested in challenging the way things are, passionately determined to understand how everything works. It is my constant sense of our feminist-sf present as a grand conversation that enables me to trace its existence into the past and from there see its trajectory extending into our future. A genealogy for feminist sf would not constitute a chart depicting direct lineages but would offer us an ever-shifting, fluid mosaic, the individual tiles of which we will probably only ever partially access. What could be more in the spirit of feminist sf than to conceptualize a genealogy that explicitly manifests our own communities across not only space but also time?

Aqueduct's small paperback series, Conversation Pieces, aims to both document and facilitate the "grand conversation." The Conversation Pieces series presents a wide variety of texts, including short fiction (which may not always be sf and may not necessarily even be feminist), essays, speeches, manifestoes, poetry, interviews, correspondence, and group discussions. Many of the texts are reprinted material, but some are new. The grand conversation reaches at least as far back as Mary Shelley and extends, in our speculations and visions, into the continually-created future. In Jonathan Goldberg's words, "To look forward to the history that will be, one must look at and retell the history that has been told." And that is what Conversation Pieces is all about.

L. Timmel Duchamp

Jonathan Goldberg, "The History That Will Be" in Louise Fradenburg and Carla Freccero, eds., *Premodern Sexualities* (New York and London: Routledge, 1996)

Published by Aqueduct Press
PO Box 95787
Seattle, WA 98145-2787
www.aqueductpress.com

 First Edition, April 2014
10 9 8 7 6 5 4 3 2 1

ISBN: 978-1-61976-057-8

All photographic collage illustrations by Katrinka Moore

Publication Acknowledgments

Otoliths: "Nothing," "Naps," "Opens," "Sees (Turns her head)," "Hatches," "Meanders," "Lingers," "Shifts (Bear)," "Rises (sun-sleepy)," "Unfolds," "Apex," "Body," "Fire," "Umbra," "Generation (river dives)," "Sees (night storm)," "Dream," "Monster," "Mingles"; photo collages on pages 2, 34, 50, 64

brevitas: "Careens," "Floats," "Water light," "Being," "Cache," "Generation (runnel to river, a small body)," "Hears," "Axis," "Generation (Restless)"

First Literary Review East: "First light," "Tangle," "Journey"

MungBeing: "Breeze," Lightning," "Scatters (unbodied)"; photo collage page 56

Möbius: "Scatters (a small body)," "Schist"

Original Block Print of Mary Shelley by Justin Kempton:
www.writersmugs.com

Printed in the USA by Applied Digital Imaging

Conversation Pieces
Volume 38

Numa

An Epic Poem
by
Katrinka Moore

for Michael and Jamie

Contents

Some, when transform'd, fix in the lasting change;
Some, more deft, thro' various figures range.

Nothing

stays / shapes
shift / becoming
always / always
in motion / nothing
settled, everlasting
shuffle & stir / in-
complete / flawed /
ravishing

I Becoming

Naps

However you imagine her, asleep
she folds in on herself fawn-like, puma
tail curled to her chin.

Opens

On a high
branch of a cedar, waxwings
nest-build — twigs, grass, fluff —
send down whistles & flickers
of light to the sleeper, who opens

her eyes. A shadow crosses as

one bird dives snatches
a tangle of shed fur &
zigzags up touching nothing.

Sees

Turns her head to the left, turns
it to the right, lifts chin, glances
up, pivots to see behind. Countless
light-arrows radiate in, drawn
from distances no one knows — no
front down back up — field
of directions leaving south east
west north in the dust.

Hatches

Numa weaves through the forest
four-legged   but wings
flap close to her temples. Slows
beneath river-bottom pines.

Clears a circle, sweeps away
needles, digs a fox hole.

(birds she's eaten   crunching
tiny bones   spitting out
beak   texture of claws)

Begins by rolling into
an egg-shape, growing
                    a shell.

bird's head on
a young girl's
body / feathery
crest, yellow-
tipped / thin fast
downy legs   hop
from one
foot to the
other / a berry
in her hand

back to her body / she
crouches / tail
switching / watches
a rowdy flock skim
the shallows / snap-
ping up dragonflies

Meanders

Ambles, pads, sniffs.   Comes
to a brake deep in ferns, dives &
tumbles under cover, soft, low, thick with
fronds. Rolls in the tangle, lies still (un-
seen) wheels, wallows.   Underbrush
sways over body invisible, so feathery
dense a layer of life carries on
at ground level, untouched until
now: smasher,   scatterer,   undulator.

Careens

down
brambled
slope, trips
over hidden
logs, skirts
snags still
standing, skids
into wet ground —
water seeps, pools,
reflects. The dark
light of the woods.

Lingers

Owl, predator herself, stays
out of reach. Nods. An
interval, silent together, as
sounds around them ebb. Child-
numen — restless — bounds —
the bird lifts off — beat of wings
& through the trees a rising
murmur buzz snort
jabber caw ululation.

Approaches

Stand
of white
birches, trunks
tilted, tops leaning on
one another, lopsided
frame : wide-open
windows, airy walls — a pushing
up, a pulling down — unhurried
balance to imbalance
hidling haven
for trial error

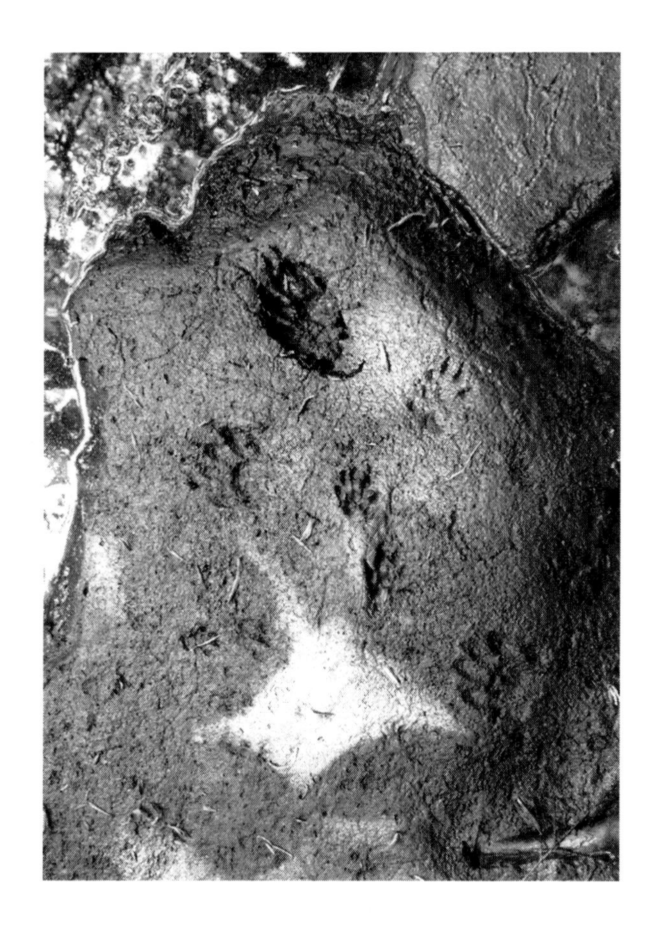

Shifts

Bear is adverse
to imitation / *careless*
numen, callow demi
god / holds with slow
honing, time biding

best to keep
a distance / try
something grand
out of sight / in
secret / ripen
ruggedize

comes out sketchy / more
critter than beast / tucked
inside rib bones, damp &
warm / knocked-about
passenger within black-
furred lumberer

blunder
has to run its course / bide

licks her fur / visceral
sediment / licks away
muck & bile / pulls
apart sticky clumps
of hair / now

sound / springs up
sanguine / hopeful /
hungry

girlchild raccoon nibbles
dew- & raspberries / rises
on hind legs / paw-
hands grabbing / this
delicious life / this
summer

Rises

sun-sleepy / she dissolves
to air / balmy, floating /
turns to wind / skims
brush / scoots around
trunks / shimmers
a thousand leaves / flies
skyward / sails / herds
cumulus / bumps
into nimbus / cools
off / drops down

Thumps

grounded / breathes
soil & sweet
rot / half-open
eyes track a black-
cherry shadow over
strands of sun / scratches
her skull on a rough-
bark stump / hears
dry beech leaves, tethered
& tossed / leaps
up / hoof fall / grazes
on stiff grass / crisp
stems, snap of grain

Ripens

eyes shut / she rolls
in red mud / fluffs
her tail / sharpens
nose / ears / waits
for light

to lower / trots
in the border-
lands / thicket,
field / half-grown
kit / forage
or frolic / track
or romp / turns
a somersault
/ pounces

Shifts

Turns her head to the left, turns
it to the right, pivots to see
behind. Deep hum among
clover & goldenrod, scattered
thistle — drone   murmur
whir. Beast-blooms buzz
& hover, field swells, lifts —

barely-flicking / Numa
nectar-sucks / unfazed
by finches digging
for seeds / clamorous
honeyers / still
in the whirling

Floats

fierce thistle / thorny / soft
purple spikes whiten / cast
off   (cloudstuff (

                                        breeze

becomes wind & scads
of seeds swirl (take her
along) fly / float / fall
                                        begin

Unfolds

burrows
under / stretches
sunward

years go
by / centuries

still / never
still / awake
from pith to
outer bark / calls
draws in / dark
anchor / needles
of light / cone

Scatters

a small body
within the open
world / unlatched

spins / each
whorl an episode
proterozoin / each

passage caught
between songs /
brushing

eolian words / a
chorus reciting
the history of air

hits earth
glances
off / sheds

Rises

sprawled on pine
needles / descends
into grace / awakes
round & bristly /
quills (hollow)

eschewed / she clambers
skyward / lodges in a
nook of pitch-trunk &
branch / celestial wind
rattles the roost / blows
notes across her spines

II Hierophanies

First light

bloom-red furrow oozes
between blue-black
sky & ash-gray
ridge / widens
warms / opens
the world / an old
old woman wakes
(again) lifts her face

Tangle

Young oak / slender
limbs / fat-lobed
baggy leaves / silhouette
on sunny barn /

just-awake child
hunkers down / snags a fine
acorn / straightens / casts
uncombed hair into
the shadow

Apex

or just
after / unclouded
light glimmers
the river / swallows
shade / silences / day
stretches / this moment

almost forever / Numa
rolls on her back / pulls heat
to her dun-colored belly

Water light

swims / stirs
cattails (light waves across (

shifts into ruffled
stalks (how she
feels to) shimmer

becomes reflection
swaying in air (inside
pond)

red-wing likeness
) wings wide (
floats down
to fluff

flies off (sky
blue water)

Body

particles eddy /
circle being-
as-light / swaddle
luminosity in
flesh and bone / in
luxury of fur
and tongue / back
to the body / familiar
wonder / Numa spills
her deep light
through mass / past
hide / out among
earthward

Breeze

clustered elms
flicker / edge
of the forest / out

in the open / on ruffled
grass / young girls struck
by the shimmering / fall
into trances / fly as they
stand / see in the dark

Fire

Circle the fire, night
at their backs. A lone
voice sings — archaic
strain — flame ashes
spiral of smoke —

Numa the darkness surrounding
them / Numa a vixen edge-
flickering / a sleepy child
catches hazel-eyed
gleam / spark

Umbra

dark travels / wind-
less / Numa spins
on her center / circles
her sister / wheels
through blackness
silence / catches
echoes distant
light / dusty red
sliver of white / passes
into shadow

at home / dolphins
take to the hills / goats
fall in love
with the waves

Crossing

Sheds heft — skin-wings
on featherbones open
to fly. Jettisons

ballast, sloughs off
gravity. Half-shut
eyes gaze outside
the world, see

Numa-as-coast
he loved as a boy.
Sea-borne winds
toss him — he
sails away.

Schist

hush / give
up breath / give
up blood / cast
off flesh / turn
fur to moss / bones
to stone / distill

flecks mingle
/ years sunder

Being

water-&-sun-washed / Numa
stretches across a moss-
patched boulder / tail dangles
groundward / sliver of sun
slips between leaves / lights
the nape of her neck / she
listens / inside   out / away
near / back   to come

III Generation

Awake

However you imagine her / awake
she leaps up / divine / weaves
through the forest / reaches
the riverbank / crouches, tail
switching / watches a merry romp —
otters — slide swim chortle

Cache

gathers stream-bank mud / molds
a little crater / for now, human
child — hands, concentration / twigs

to stick on the outside / moss
to line the inside / when the mud
dries / the nest set / she hides

it / cached in its hollow
a river-glazed stone / a
hawk's red feather

Generation

river-dives / surfaces
sleek-furred / falls
in with a rollicking
clan / water-chase
& wrestle / toss &
juggle sun-white bone /
slide-mud splash &
whistle / Numa flirts
with a frisky pup / they
roll on their own / baby-
making / hiss   purr   growl
squall   /   hum

~

runnel to river / Numa climbs
against its course / attends
to pathways / soil, stone / sniffs
scouts   uncovers / high on the
ridge-side / boulder-screened
burrow / grotto of inner
space / lair   den   nursery

~

a small body within
the open world / unlatched
/ moored inside an orb
of legs, torso, tail / milk
sleepy / breath brims,
ebbs / absorbed
by being

IV Interloper

Sees

night storm / a tall pine
upends, sprawls across
an ephemeral pool, hatches
an emptiness that sunlight
fills / root bed uncovered,
muddle of moss rock mud, a few
trapped feathers, speckled,
still soft, still smooth / Numa
lifts her face to the warmth, half-
shut eyes, apparition

Dream

A distant boy dreams   dangerous nights
pale clouds course   across the sky
stillness below.   A boulder topples
& hurtles down   hews an artery
through ancient trees.   Transformed amid
the vestiges   he jettisons
his qualms and fights.   Defeats — alone —
an umbrous demon.   This dusky world
that lies outside   all ordinary ebb
& flow, goads him   to glory-seek.

Hears

rumor whispers
tales / come
on air / shedding
feathers / come
true some-
how / some-
thing / some-
body's coming /
interloper

Journey

He strives against wind   over waterless dunes
sandblind & solitary.   Sand-shuffles
on shifting terrain.   Enticing music —
singing, strumming —   summons the seeker
& leads him astray.   Lost, deceived
by invisible voices   vying & calling
his name, he stumbles.   Gnarled, afraid,
he wills himself   to walk, shun
fears, leave hope   behind. He stuffs
his ears. Set free   earth-bound
he follows his bones   beat of the heart.

Labyrinth

Exultant, frightened
he enters the forest.   His footsteps
set off calls & hoots.   A chorus of
cries drowns out   the crackling leaves —
dead & dried   covering dirt, hiding
entrances, exits   escape routes —
a labyrinth of lives   led without
him, without knowing   his ways.

Stalks

Numa races / slips
under low-slung
branches / dodges
outcrops / weaves
through thickets /
saplings / leaps
logs / breaks / silent /
lopes fast full
loops / wider
circles / leaves
no trail / makes no
sound / hears each
move / hears
trespassing

Monster

He seeks a monster
to meet & challenge.   Chances upon
the numen, protean   nymph-animal —
no breath of fire   no fearsome talons
no sword-proof scales.   Scaddle creature,
circler, unguarded   guardian, wordless
messenger, *monstrum*   omen, vessel.

Leads (astray)

she nestles / oak
hollow / wakes
up clattery / sprints
up airy sprigs / tracks
intruder who mis-
reads insults as
invitation / follows
her deep into
hemlocks / far
from the stream / far
from a path / from any
route outside / there
she abandons him

Doubt

Tricked, diminished   he doubts his quest
laughs at his longing   to live as a hero
now only longs   to live. And so
he wills himself   to wake, find
food, make   fire, survive.

And so he begins   to gather vines,
braid stems to make   a strand of rope.
Slips knot to form   a sling.

Meander

Amble, pad, sniff. The whelp wheels, tumbles through, hides in the tangle, pounces — till Numa draws up: stand of slow-falling birches, airy walls, grassy nest. She curls up egg-like, her cub copies. Two shells grow, crack open. Full-fledged owl flies to a low branch. Hatchling (tiny cat paws) clings to a flimsy stalk.

Amble, pad, sniff. Whim-chaser romps to water, river-dives, wallows in muddy edges, ripples, takes on algae, settles in. Numa crouches on land, watches for herons.

End of practice, offspring springs up, hopeful, hungry. Numa tramples leaves, grabs a stick, shifts into glory-seeker — the cub a fierce boy with a cougar tail. Back to their bodies, two cats roll on the riverbank, laughing.

Lightning

He is learning to live isolated, in shadow
in the span between trunks in the space beneath branches
under light-sifting leaves. One late afternoon
in a low-angle glint he glimpses a path —
or thinks he does. In a thicket of laurel
he traces the trail tracks through the duskscape
as cumuli billow become thunderheads
choke off the remnants of rays. The path
limned by slashes of lightning, unflagging
he reaches a ridge wrests free of the tangle
stands still & waits for a streak, for a flare
waits as the wind waxes and bays
as the rain teems and the river rises.

Jagged light bolts & below, he sees
a beast or a stump boulder or vision.
Loads stone into sling and lets it fly
hurls it as lightning licks down, splits
an oak, thud echoed by thunder.

The boy runs headlong away from the havoc
(hero or sinner assassin or coward)
runs without seeing runs till the rain stops
the clouds move apart and the moon breaks through.

now sun reaches through light-sifting leaves / clouds
spread across the late afternoon sky

under light-sifting leaves
remnants of rays
in the late afternoon

now thunderheads billow / block remnants
of rays / wind whispers and ripens / a
thunderclap bellows

inkling of rain
wind whistles and heightens
lightning streaks through
streaming-down rain

Numa scruff-carries cub (streaks beneath
lightning) up the side of the ridge

carries scruffy wet cub
to the boulder-screened burrow
in the side of the ridge

leaves her fledgling inside the dry, hidden burrow / returns
to the fray

leaves flurry / limbs slap / river rushes

Numa returns to the fray / umbrous & troubled

wide river rushes

she steals through the wildness / umbrous & troubled
freezes beneath a high-branching oak

breathes in the wildness

now lightning fractures the high-branching
oak / crack echoing thunder

now lightning fractures
Numa crumples
thunder cracks

the storm passes over numen-as-stillness
/ being-as-nothing

clouds move apart
the storm passes on
the moon breaks through

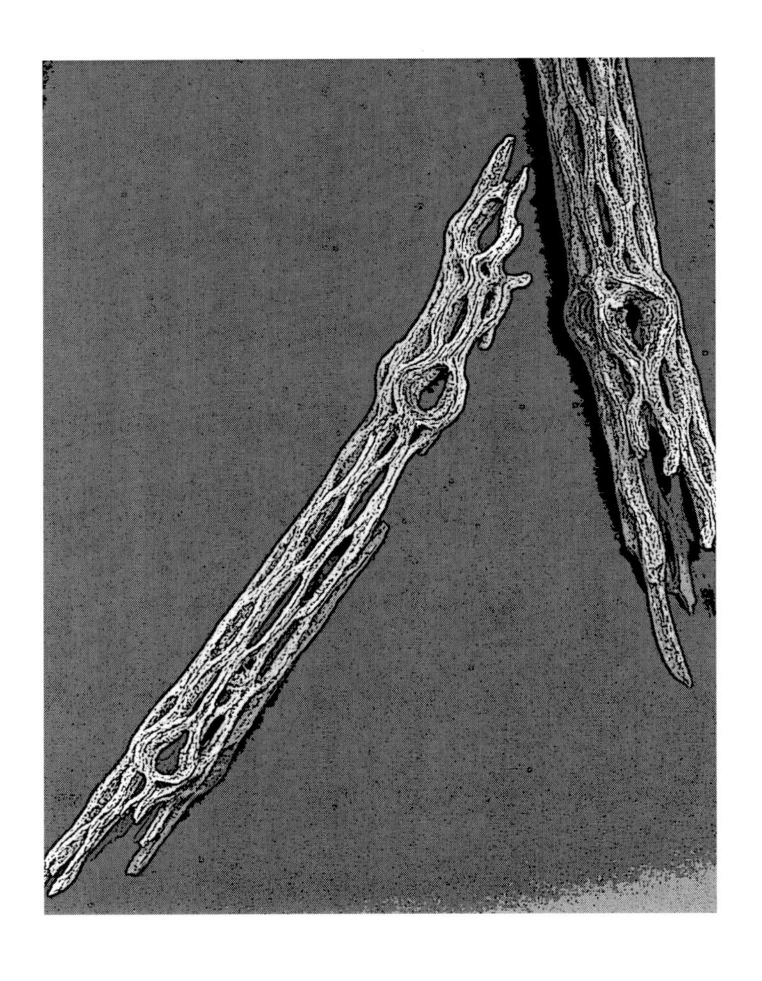

Mingles

sleeps on the bank & in early
morning soaks up fallen
rain / draws it in past fur, through
hide / till she spills over / follows
a furrow / enters the river / mingles /
Numa's drunk in, swallowed / becomes
wetness & motion / takes the tint
of the sky / gives up her old being

unbodied / atoms / longing / cycle / exile / sorrow

Axis

rumor whispers
tales / it wasn't
the tree but
they said it
was / amounts
to the same
thing / line
from heaven
to earth / severed
cut into pieces

Generation

Restless, the cub slips out
out of the den into the light
light-treads through ferns and brush
brushes the air close to earth.
Earth opens under outstretched roots —
roots that obscure
an obscure cache.
Cached in this hollow, nesting,
a nest of treasures, gleaned
(gleam of river, echo of shadow).

Shadowing mother, she changes, returns
returns & changes. Shifts to fathom
thrum of all things, everlasting hum.
Hums a low note, rolls over, rests.

Epilogue

The hero lingers   later, after —
hearing breeze-   batted leaves
clacking bare   branches, rustle
of underbrush   bracken whispers —
honed, obscure   till old with hope.

People pick   at the periphery
tentative, trying   to determine
the consequences.

Scatters

unbodied / atoms / longing / cycle / exile / sorrow

river escapes the storm-shifted
forest / flows fast, wide / ferries
remnants / deepens hollows
/ spills down slopes / enters
the prairie / slows snakes
winds / smooth skin of sky /
drawn to desert / dwindles / casts
sediment (earthbound, holy)
over rock & sand

Rises

disassembled / how to
corral heart / knit
breath blood /

scattered in detritus / strewn
(hidden) scraps, some
already nipped by quick-
witted gnatcatchers / Numa
calls / concocts her
self (each cell burns)
gathers rind and bone

she calls / corrals / becomes / begins again

Notes

The epigraph is taken from Ovid's *Metamorphoses,* Book VIII, translated by Thomas Vernon.

"Lingers" A *numen* is a local divinity; here, one that shape-shifts.

Hierophanies are objects or events that are revelations of the sacred.

"Umbra" The image of dolphins and land animals changing places in the wake of an eclipse comes from Archilochos' poem about the total eclipse of the sun in 648 BCE.

Many thanks to my sister, Nancy Jane Moore, the
One O'clock Poets—Elizabeth Poreba, Sarah Stern,
Martie Palar, Joan Poole, Maura Candela, Katie Johntz,
Guillermo Castro, Ron Drummond, John Couturier—
and Holly Anderson and Caroline Beasley-Baker

Author Biography

Katrinka Moore is the author of two previous poetry collections, *Thief* and *This is Not a Story* (winner of the Finishing Line Press New Women's Voices Prize). She has poems in the anthologies *This Full Green Hour, The Best of the Texas Poetry Calendar,* and Milkweed Editions' *Stories from Where We Live.* Her work has appeared in *MungBeing, Otoliths, Dépositions le blog, First Literary Review-East,* and other journals. A former choreographer and dancer, she grew up in rural Texas and lives in New York.